Instagram marketing for fashion

Unlock the Power of Social Media to Skyrocket Your Fashion Brand

Sharon.s Candelaria

Table of Contents

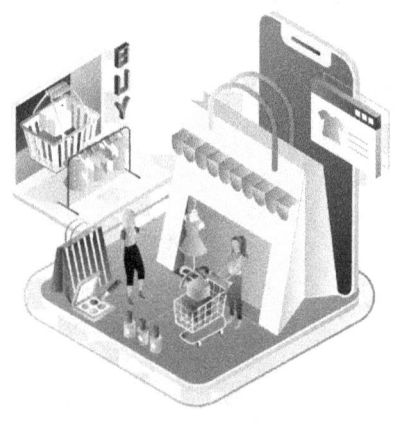

Introduction

Welcome to the world of Instagram marketing for fashion! If you're a fashion enthusiast, a budding designer, or a fashion brand looking to make a mark in the digital realm, you've come to the right place. Instagram has become a powerhouse platform for fashion, where trends are born, styles are celebrated, and brands connect with their passionate followers.

Imagine having a virtual runway at your fingertips, where you can showcase your latest collections, share behind-the-scenes glimpses of your creative process, and engage directly with your audience. With Instagram, you can transform your fashion aspirations into a visual feast that captivates and inspires.

But it's not just about posting pretty pictures. Instagram marketing for fashion requires a strategic approach. It's about weaving a compelling narrative, curating an enticing feed, and building an authentic community of fashion enthusiasts who eagerly await your next creation.

In this journey, we'll delve into the art of creating a captivating profile that speaks volumes about your brand. We'll explore the importance of stunning visuals, from striking photos to captivating videos, that will make your fashion pieces come alive on the small screen. We'll uncover the power of consistent branding, where your unique style and voice shine through every post.

And let's not forget about the secret weapon of Instagram success: hashtags. We'll unlock the mysteries of choosing the right hashtags to amplify your reach, attract new followers, and connect with fashion influencers who can help propel your brand to new heights.

So, whether you're an aspiring fashion blogger, a boutique owner seeking to expand your online presence, or an established fashion brand looking to leverage the full potential of Instagram, fasten your seatbelts and get ready to explore the captivating world of Instagram marketing for fashion. Your journey to fashion stardom starts now!

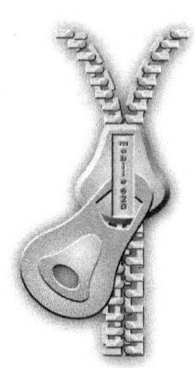

Instagram market for fashion

Instagram has become one of the most popular social media platforms for businesses, especially in the fashion and parts industries. With its visual nature and vast user base, Instagram offers a unique opportunity to showcase products, engage with customers, and drive sales. This comprehensive guide will provide valuable insights and strategies to leverage Instagram marketing effectively in the fashion and parts sectors.

1. Establishing Your Instagram Presence:

- Create a Business Account: Switch to a business account to access analytics, insights, and advertising features.
- Optimize Your Profile: Craft a compelling bio, use a recognizable profile picture, and include relevant links and contact information.

2. Content Strategy:

- Visual Appeal: High-quality images and videos are crucial for fashion and parts brands. Showcase your products in an aesthetically pleasing and aspirational manner.
- Consistency: Develop a consistent visual theme and tone of voice that aligns with your brand identity.
- User-Generated Content (UGC): Encourage customers to share their experiences with your products by reposting their content, using appropriate hashtags and giving credit.

3. Hashtags and Trend Discovery:

- Research Relevant Hashtags: Identify industry-specific and trending hashtags related to fashion and parts. Tools like Instagram's search function and third-party platforms can assist in finding popular tags.

- Branded Hashtags: Create a unique branded hashtag to encourage user engagement and increase brand visibility.

- Trend Discovery: Stay updated on the latest trends, styles, and conversations in the fashion and parts industries. Participate in relevant challenges and conversations to boost engagement.

4. Influencer Partnerships:

- Identify Influencers: Collaborate with influencers whose audience aligns with your target market. Look for engagement rates, authenticity, and relevance.

- Product Placements and Reviews: Send your products to influencers for them to feature in their content. Reviews and endorsements from trusted influencers can greatly impact purchasing decisions.

- Sponsored Posts: Consider sponsored posts to amplify your reach and increase brand awareness.

5. Engaging with Your Audience:

- Respond to Comments: Reply to comments and messages promptly, providing exceptional customer service and building a loyal customer base.
- Run Contests and Giveaways: Organize contests and giveaways to encourage user participation and generate excitement around your brand.
- Instagram Stories: Utilize features like polls, questions, and swipe-up links in Instagram Stories to engage with your audience in real-time.

6. Instagram Advertising:

- Boosted Posts: Amplify your content's reach by using the "Boost" feature on Instagram. Target specific demographics, locations, and interests to maximize effectiveness.
- Instagram Ads: Utilize Instagram's ad platform to create targeted campaigns that

drive traffic, increase conversions, and promote your fashion or parts products.

7. Analytics and Insights:

- Track Performance: Regularly monitor Instagram analytics to evaluate the success of your marketing efforts. Analyze engagement rates, follower growth, reach, and post-performance.

- Adjust Your Strategy: Use data-driven insights to optimize your content strategy, posting schedule, and advertising campaigns.

Conclusion

Instagram marketing presents a valuable opportunity for fashion and parts businesses to connect with their target audience, build brand awareness, and drive sales. By implementing the strategies outlined in this comprehensive guide, you can leverage the power of Instagram to showcase your products, engage with customers, and stay ahead of the competition in these competitive industries. Remember to adapt and refine your approach based on analytics and insights to ensure continued success on the platform.

About The Author

Sharon S. Candelaria, a dynamic entrepreneur, investor, and online business expert, is reshaping the landscape of financial success for aspiring entrepreneurs worldwide. With her passion for empowering others, Sharon has become a trusted mentor, guiding over 300 students towards financial independence and online business mastery.

Recognized for her remarkable achievements at such a young age, Sharon's expertise lies in leveraging the power of the digital realm to generate passive income and build thriving online businesses. Her extensive knowledge spans various domains, including e-commerce, affiliate marketing, dropshipping, and social media advertising. By dissecting complex strategies into actionable steps, she has empowered countless individuals to turn their passions into profitable ventures.

Sharon's ability to navigate the ever-evolving online business landscape sets her apart as a true industry leader. Her innovative thinking and entrepreneurial flair have led her to uncover unique investment opportunities, enabling her students to achieve remarkable results. With her guidance, they have unlocked financial freedom and embraced a lifestyle unbound by traditional limitations.

Beyond her entrepreneurial pursuits, Sharon's dedication to teaching and mentoring stems from a deep-rooted belief in the power of education. Through her engaging speaking engagements, workshops, and online courses, she imparts practical knowledge and fosters a supportive community that encourages personal and professional growth.

Join Sharon S. Candelaria's growing community of successful entrepreneurs and take charge of your financial future,and embark on a journey towards unlimited possibilities today.

Project Name: Priority: ☐ ☐ ☐ ☐ ☐

Date: Difficulty: ☐ ☐ ☐ ☐ ☐

Description: Ideas:

Materials:
- ☐
- ☐
- ☐
- ☐
- ☐
- ☐
- ☐
- ☐
- ☐
- ☐

Sketches:

Notes:

Project Name:

Date:

Priority: ☐ ☐ ☐ ☐ ☐

Difficulty: ☐ ☐ ☐ ☐ ☐

Description:

Ideas:

Materials:

☐ _____

☐ _____

☐ _____

☐ _____

☐ _____

☐ _____

☐ _____

☐ _____

☐ _____

☐ _____

Sketches:

Notes:

Project Name:

Date:

Priority: ☐ ☐ ☐ ☐ ☐

Difficulty: ☐ ☐ ☐ ☐ ☐

Description:

Ideas:

Materials:

- ☐
- ☐
- ☐
- ☐
- ☐
- ☐
- ☐
- ☐
- ☐
- ☐

Sketches:

Notes:

Project Name:

Date:

Priority: ☐ ☐ ☐ ☐ ☐

Difficulty: ☐ ☐ ☐ ☐ ☐

Description:

Ideas:

Materials:

☐
☐
☐
☐
☐
☐
☐
☐
☐

Notes:

Sketches:

Project Name:

Date:

Priority: ☐ ☐ ☐ ☐ ☐

Difficulty: ☐ ☐ ☐ ☐ ☐

Description:

_____

_____

_____

_____

_____

_____

Ideas:

Materials:

☐ _____

☐ _____

☐ _____

☐ _____

☐ _____

☐ _____

☐ _____

☐ _____

☐ _____

☐ _____

Sketches:

Notes:

_____

_____

_____

_____

_____

Project Name:　　　　　　Priority: ☐ ☐ ☐ ☐ ☐

Date:　　　　　　　　　　Difficulty: ☐ ☐ ☐ ☐ ☐

Description:　　　　　　　Ideas:

_____

_____

_____

_____

_____

_____

Materials:

☐ _____

☐ _____

☐ _____

☐ _____

☐ _____

☐ _____

☐ _____

☐ _____

☐ _____

☐ _____

Notes:　　　　　　　　　Sketches:

_____

_____

_____

_____

_____

_____

Project Name: Priority: ☐ ☐ ☐ ☐ ☐

Date: Difficulty: ☐ ☐ ☐ ☐ ☐

Description: Ideas:

_____

_____

_____

_____

_____

_____

Materials:

☐ _____

☐ _____

☐ _____

☐ _____

☐ _____   Sketches:

☐ _____

☐ _____

☐ _____

☐ _____

☐ _____

Notes:

_____

_____

_____

_____

_____

_____

Project Name: Priority: ☐ ☐ ☐ ☐ ☐

Date: Difficulty: ☐ ☐ ☐ ☐ ☐

Description:

Ideas:

Materials:

- ☐
- ☐
- ☐
- ☐
- ☐
- ☐
- ☐
- ☐
- ☐
- ☐

Sketches:

Notes:

Project Name: Priority: ☐ ☐ ☐ ☐ ☐

Date: Difficulty: ☐ ☐ ☐ ☐ ☐

Description: Ideas:

_____

_____

_____

_____

_____

Materials:
☐ _____
☐ _____
☐ _____
☐ _____
☐ _____   Sketches:
☐ _____
☐ _____
☐ _____
☐ _____
☐ _____

Notes:

_____

_____

_____

_____

_____

Project Name: Priority: ☐ ☐ ☐ ☐ ☐

Date: Difficulty: ☐ ☐ ☐ ☐ ☐

Description: Ideas:

_____

_____

_____

_____

_____

_____

Materials:

☐ _____

☐ _____

☐ _____

☐ _____

☐ _____   Sketches:

☐ _____

☐ _____

☐ _____

☐ _____

Notes:

_____

_____

_____

_____

_____

www.ingramcontent.com/pod-product-compliance
Lightning Source LLC
Chambersburg PA
CBHW072227290526
45794CB00007B/2921